Cool CLEAN JOKES *For Kids!*

BOB PHILLIPS

HARVEST HOUSE PUBLISHERS
Eugene, Oregon 97402

To
Tyler Scott—
who is a great
joy to my heart

TOTALLY COOL CLEAN JOKES FOR KIDS

Eugene, Oregon 97402
ISBN 1-56507-571-4

Printed in the United States of America.

97 98 99 00 01 02 /LP/ 10 9 8 7 6 5 4 3 2 1

Contents

1

Harlow & Hector

Harlow: What do you get if you cross a pig with a small dog?
Hector: I have no idea.
Harlow: A piginese.

❖ ❖ ❖

Harlow: What do you get when you cross a comedy with a gardening show?
Hector: Who knows?
Harlow: Jokes you can really dig.

❖ ❖ ❖

Harlow: What do they call it when atomic scientists grab their rods and gather around the old watering hole?

Hector: I don't have the foggiest.
Harlow: Nuclear fishin'.

❖ ❖ ❖

Harlow: What word is pronounced differently when capitalized?
Hector: You tell me.
Harlow: Polish and polish.

❖ ❖ ❖

Harlow: What's green and bores holes?
Hector: I can't guess.
Harlow: A drill pickle.

❖ ❖ ❖

Harlow: What's orange, good for your eyes, and jumps out of airplanes?
Hector: My mind is a blank.
Harlow: Carrot-troopers.

❖ ❖ ❖

Harlow: What do you get when a steamroller runs over a tomato, a pepper, and a pickle?
Hector: I give up.
Harlow: Relish.

❖ ❖ ❖

Harlow: What did the fog bank say after somebody tried to hit it?
Hector: That's a mystery.
Harlow: You mist me.

❖ ❖ ❖

Harlow: What does a pig do when he reads a book in bed?
Hector: I'm a blank.
Harlow: He curls up with his favorite tail.

❖ ❖ ❖

Harlow: What are you doing with those art supplies?
Hector: I'm going to draw my own conclusions.

❖ ❖ ❖

Harlow: What do you do when an actor gives a bad performance in Hungary?
Hector: I'm in the dark.
Harlow: You boodepest.

2

Nole & David

Nole: Where do pigs live?
David: I pass.
Nole: In a high grime area.

❖ ❖ ❖

Nole: Where are the Himalayas?
David: You've got me guessing.
Nole: If you'd put things away, you'd know where to find them.

❖ ❖ ❖

Nole: Where do continents put their plates when they're through eating?
David: How should I know?
Nole: On the Continental Shelf.

❖ ❖ ❖

Nole: Where do spies do their shopping?
David: Search me.
Nole: At the snooper market.

❖ ❖ ❖

Nole: Where do pigs go for an exotic vacation?
David: I have no clue.
Nole: To the Sow Pacific.

❖ ❖ ❖

Nole: Where does Santa Claus stay when he goes on vacation?
David: I don't know.
Nole: In a ho-ho-tel.

❖ ❖ ❖

Nole: Where is medicine first mentioned in the Bible?
David: I give up.
Nole: When the Lord gives Moses two tablets.

❖ ❖ ❖

Nole: Where does a snail eat?
David: I have no idea.
Nole: In a slow-food restaurant.

❖ ❖ ❖

Nole: Where do squirrels live?
David: Who knows?
Nole: In nut houses.

❖ ❖ ❖

Nole: Where do mountains cook their food?
David: I don't have the foggiest.
Nole: On mountain ranges.

❖ ❖ ❖

Nole: Where did the homeless peach end up?
David: You tell me.
Nole: In the pits.

❖ ❖ ❖

Nole: Where was deviled ham mentioned in the Bible?
David: I can't guess.
Nole: When the evil spirits entered the swine.

❖ ❖ ❖

Nole: Where was the Declaration of Independence signed?
David: My mind is a blank.
Nole: At the bottom of the paper.

3

Blinda & Benedick

Blinda: Wasn't it sad . . . that movie about the whale?
Benedick: No.
Blinda: Well, it really made me blubber.

❖ ❖ ❖

Blinda: Are you a light sleeper?
Benedick: Yes, I am a very light sleeper.
Blinda: I'm not, I sleep in the dark.

❖ ❖ ❖

Blinda: Guess what? I got two orders today!
Benedick: Congratulations! What were they?
Blinda: "Get out!" and "Stay out!"

❖ ❖ ❖

Blinda: Did you hear about the customer who bought a chicken that didn't have a wish bone?

Benedick: No, what happened?

Blinda: The butcher told the customer that his chickens are so happy they have nothing to wish for.

❖ ❖ ❖

Blinda: Did you hear the story about the cop who asked his partner why he didn't say a word during the entire police movie they went to see?

Benedick: No, what did he say?

Blinda: He said he had the right to remain silent.

❖ ❖ ❖

Blinda: I wish there was something we could do about all this noise pollution.

Benedick: Well, we could start with you not talking so much.

❖ ❖ ❖

Blinda: Which two states are run by ducks?

Benedick: I give up.

Blinda: North Duckota and South Duckota.

❖ ❖ ❖

Blinda: Which do you think is more important, the sun or the moon?

Benedick: I don't have a clue.

Blinda: I think it would be the moon. The nights would be too dark without its light, but the sun shines by day, so we don't need it then.

❖ ❖ ❖

Blinda: One of the members of my family thinks he's a pen.

Benedick: You're kidding me.

Blinda: Yes, it's true. He's my Bic brother.

❖ ❖ ❖

Blinda: I think his name should be Lumberjack.

Benedick: Why?

Blinda: He looks like a good feller.

❖ ❖ ❖

Blinda: Let's go with my first suggestion.

Benedick: But I have an idea!

Blinda: That's beginner's luck.

❖ ❖ ❖

Blinda: If a man is living in Winston Salem, North Carolina, can he be buried west of the Mississippi?
Benedick: You've got me guessing.
Blinda: Not if he's living.

4

Doctor, Doctor

Patient: Doctor, my husband thinks he's an anchor. Is there any hope for him?
Doctor: Nope. He's sunk!

❖ ❖ ❖

Patient: Doctor, my sister thinks she's a picnic lunch.
Doctor: She sounds like a basket case to me.

❖ ❖ ❖

Doctor: Take one of these pills once a day for the rest of your life.
Patient: But there's only seven pills in this bottle.
Doctor: I know.

❖ ❖ ❖

Patient: Doctor, my father thinks he's a tree.

Doctor: We'd better nip this in the bud.

❖ ❖ ❖

Patient: Doctor, everyone tries to take advantage of me. What should I do?

Doctor: Give me 200 dollars and let me borrow your car.

❖ ❖ ❖

Patient: Doctor, doctor, I keep thinking I'm the Abominable Snowman.

Doctor: Sorry, I don't get your drift.

❖ ❖ ❖

Wife: Doctor, doctor, my husband thinks he's a shepherd!

Doctor: Don't lose any sheep over it.

❖ ❖ ❖

Patient: Doctor, what can you give me for my kleptomania?

Doctor: How about Klepto-Bismol?

❖ ❖ ❖

Patient: Doctor, doctor, I have a ringing in my ears! What should I do?
Doctor: Get an unlisted number.

❖ ❖ ❖

Patient: Doctor, my uncle thinks he's a tube of glue.
Doctor: He must be losing his grip on reality.

❖ ❖ ❖

1st patient: Did you hear about the dentist who tried to give an injection of novocaine to a rabbit?
2nd patient: No, what happened?
1st patient: The rabbit cried, "Not the needle! I'm the ether bunny!"

5

Patsy & Peggy

Patsy: Why did the dimwit fall on his knee to cough?

Peggy: I give up.

Patsy: His doctor prescribed a cough drop.

❖ ❖ ❖

Patsy: Why is a room full of married people always empty?

Peggy: I have no idea.

Patsy: There's not a single person in it.

❖ ❖ ❖

Patsy: Why did the director fire the elephant?

Peggy: Who knows?

Patsy: He kept throwing his weight around.

❖ ❖ ❖

Patsy: Why didn't the last dove return to the Ark?
Peggy: I don't have the foggiest.
Patsy: She had sufficient grounds to stay away.

❖ ❖ ❖

Patsy: Why did the axe go to the doctor?
Peggy: You tell me.
Patsy: For a splitting headache.

❖ ❖ ❖

Patsy: Why is a man who is always complaining the easiest man to satisfy?
Peggy: I can't guess.
Patsy: Nothing satisfies him.

❖ ❖ ❖

Patsy: Why should you add extra letter "L's" to a story?
Peggy: My mind is a blank.
Patsy: There should be a more-L to every story.

❖ ❖ ❖

Patsy: Why did Moses cross the Red Sea?
Peggy: I give up.
Patsy: To avoid Egyptian traffic.

❖ ❖ ❖

Patsy: Why did the fan write the baseball player a long letter?
Peggy: That's a mystery.
Patsy: One pitcher is worth a thousand words.

❖ ❖ ❖

Patsy: Why was Adam's first day the longest?
Peggy: I'm a blank.
Patsy: It had no Eve.

❖ ❖ ❖

Patsy: Why did Mickey Mouse go to outer space?
Peggy: It's unknown to me.
Patsy: To find Pluto.

❖ ❖ ❖

Patsy: Why did the moron jump in the swimming pool fully clothed?
Peggy: I'm in the dark.
Patsy: He wanted to go skin-diving and he needed a wet suit.

❖ ❖ ❖

Patsy: Why can't you put an old-fashioned pig into a pit?

Peggy: I pass.
Patsy: You can't fit a square pig into a round hole.

6

Amelia & Argus

Amelia: What do astronauts do when they're dirty?

Argus: I give up.

Amelia: Take a meteor shower.

❖ ❖ ❖

Amelia: What do you get when you cross jumbo vegetables and wheat?

Argus: I have no idea.

Amelia: The Jolly Grain Giant.

❖ ❖ ❖

Amelia: What kind of fish do you find in a bird cage?

Argus: Who knows?
Amelia: A perch.

❖ ❖ ❖

Amelia: What's green, has four legs and six pockets, and would probably kill you if it fell out of a tree?
Argus: I don't have the foggiest.
Amelia: A pool table.

❖ ❖ ❖

Amelia: What's the difference between a redneck and a pig?
Argus: You tell me.
Amelia: One likes to eat, sleep, belch, and roll in the mud. The other is considered intelligent and has a curly tail and a flat snout.

❖ ❖ ❖

Amelia: What do you get when you cross a news show with a cooking show?
Argus: I can't guess.
Amelia: A lot of hot scoops.

❖ ❖ ❖

Amelia: What do you call stories about strange, ancient Smogarian heroes?

Argus: My mind is a blank.
Amelia: Geek mythology.

❖ ❖ ❖

Amelia: What do you call a cow that plays the violin?
Argus: I give up.
Amelia: Fiddler on the Hoof.

❖ ❖ ❖

Amelia: What do you call killer bees who help in undercover police work?
Argus: That's a mystery.
Amelia: A sting operation.

❖ ❖ ❖

Amelia: What does a gorilla wear when he cooks?
Argus: I'm a blank.
Amelia: His ape-ron.

❖ ❖ ❖

Amelia: What do you call a doctor who lives in Egypt?
Argus: It's unknown to me.
Amelia: A Cairo-practor.

❖ ❖ ❖

Amelia: What do you get when you stick your tongue out at a tornado?
Argus: I'm in the dark.
Amelia: A tongue-twister.

❖ ❖ ❖

Amelia: What would you call it if worms took over the world?
Argus: I pass.
Amelia: Global worming.

7

Who's There?

Knock, knock.
Who's there?
Ron.
Ron who?
Ron fast. Here comes a wild tiger!

❖ ❖ ❖

Knock, knock.
Who's there?
Aware.
Aware who?
Aware, aware have my little sheep gone?

❖ ❖ ❖

Knock, knock.
Who's there?
Isaac.
Isaac who?
Isaac. Call a doctor.

❖ ❖ ❖

Knock, knock.
Who's there?
Chimney.
Chimney who?
Chimney cricket! Have you seen Pinocchio?

❖ ❖ ❖

Knock, knock.
Who's there?
Ammonia.
Ammonia who?
Ammonia bird in a gilded cage.

❖ ❖ ❖

Knock, knock.
Who's there?
Tibet.
Tibet who?
Early tibet, early to rise, makes a man healthy, wealthy and wise.

❖ ❖ ❖

Knock, knock.
Who's there?
Summons.
Summons who?
Summons at the door knocking.

❖ ❖ ❖

Knock, knock.
Who's there?
Egypt.
Egypt who?
Egypt me a quarter on this ice cream cone.

❖ ❖ ❖

Knock, knock.
Who's there?
Justin.
Justin who?
Justin time for the evening news.

❖ ❖ ❖

Knock, knock.
Who's there?
Formosa.
Formosa who?
Formosa the day I was in the principal's office.

❖ ❖ ❖

Knock, knock.
Who's there?
Weirdo.
Weirdo who?
Weirdo the deer and the antelopes play?

❖ ❖ ❖

Knock, knock.
Who's there?
August.
August who?
August wind.

8

Tyler & Eric

Tyler: Where do cows go on dates?
Eric: I give up.
Tyler: To the moovies.

❖ ❖ ❖

Tyler: Where do you write the word "lily"?
Eric: I have no idea.
Tyler: On a lily pad.

❖ ❖ ❖

Tyler: Where does the Abominable Snow Pig live?
Eric: Who knows?
Tyler: In the Hamalayas.

❖ ❖ ❖

Tyler: Where does a lumberjack write things down?
Eric: I don't have the foggiest.
Tyler: In his log book.

❖ ❖ ❖

Tyler: Where did Noah strike the first nail in the ark?
Eric: You tell me.
Tyler: On the head.

❖ ❖ ❖

Tyler: Where is tennis mentioned in the Bible?
Eric: I can't guess.
Tyler: When Joseph served in Pharaoh's court.

❖ ❖ ❖

Tyler: Where do Eskimos keep their sled dogs?
Eric: My mind is a blank.
Tyler: In a mushroom.

❖ ❖ ❖

Tyler: Where does sour cream come from?
Eric: I give up.
Tyler: Discontented cows.

❖ ❖ ❖

Tyler: Where does a lumberjack go to have fun?
Eric: That's a mystery.
Tyler: To a tree-ring circus.

❖ ❖ ❖

Tyler: Where do ecologists get their mail?
Eric: I'm a blank.
Tyler: At the com-post office.

❖ ❖ ❖

Tyler: Where would you find a homeless octopus?
Eric: It's unknown to me.
Tyler: On squid row.

9

Angelo & Alpheus

Angelo: Did you hear about the boy who asked to speak to the Invisible Man?

Alpheus: No, tell me.

Angelo: His mother told him she hadn't seen him around.

❖ ❖ ❖

Angelo: Hey, look at this great watch I found in the street.

Alpheus: Are you sure it was lost?

Angelo: Of course it was lost. I saw the guy looking for it.

❖ ❖ ❖

Angelo: I overheard a conversation between the pastor and a visitor of the church. The pastor said to the visitor, "Isn't this a beautiful church? Here is a plaque for the men who died in the service."

Alpheus: What did the visitor say?

Angelo: The man said, "Which one? . . . Morning or evening?"

❖ ❖ ❖

Angelo: Which foods are especially good for young people?

Alpheus: I don't have the foggiest.

Angelo: The pro-teens!

❖ ❖ ❖

Angelo: I feel like my aunt likes to mother me.

Alpheus: I noticed that.

Angelo: Yeah. She's becoming more of a parent every day.

❖ ❖ ❖

Angelo: I can tie a rope.

Alpheus: Show me how you do it.

Angelo: Knot now.

❖ ❖ ❖

Angelo: I bet you don't know what a space probe is.

Alpheus: No I don't, what is it?

Angelo: It's what the doctor uses when he looks in your ears.

❖ ❖ ❖

Angelo: Can a horse testify in court?

Alpheus: I give up.

Angelo: Yes, if it's under oats.

❖ ❖ ❖

Angelo: Which is easier to hunt, leopards or tigers?

Alpheus: That's a mystery.

Angelo: Leopards. They're easier to spot.

❖ ❖ ❖

Angelo: Can you read Chinese?

Alpheus: No, can you?

Angelo: Yes, but only when it's printed in English.

❖ ❖ ❖

Angelo: I have two brand-new computers.

Alpheus: Why did you purchase two?

Angelo: The sales clerk said it would do half of my work for me. So, I bought two so they would do all of my work for me.

❖ ❖ ❖

Angelo: Can you hang a man in Texas with a wooden leg?
Alpheus: I'm in the dark.
Angelo: They usually hang a man with a rope.

❖ ❖ ❖

Angelo: I finally trained my dog not to beg at the table.
Alpheus: How did you do that?
Angelo: I let him taste my sister's cooking.

❖ ❖ ❖

Angelo: At what season did Eve eat the fruit?
Alpheus: You've got me guessing.
Angelo: Early in the fall.

❖ ❖ ❖

Angelo: Did you hear about the customer who asked the waiter what a fly was doing in his soup?
Alpheus: No, what happened?
Angelo: The waiter said, "Looks like the cha-cha-cha."

10

Eugenia & Tammy

Eugenia: Why did the barber move to Hawaii?
Tammy: I give up.
Eugenia: He wanted to become a beachcomber.

❖ ❖ ❖

Eugenia: Why shouldn't you tell a giraffe a secret?
Tammy: I have no idea.
Eugenia: You might strain yourself climbing up to whisper in its ear.

❖ ❖ ❖

Eugenia: Why wouldn't the centipede dance with the elephant?
Tammy: Who knows?

Eugenia: It was afraid of getting its feet stepped on.

❖ ❖ ❖

Eugenia: Why don't people ever mention the number 288?

Tammy: I don't have the foggiest.

Eugenia: It's two gross.

❖ ❖ ❖

Eugenia: Why was the pig thrown out of the football game?

Tammy: You tell me.

Eugenia: He played dirty.

❖ ❖ ❖

Eugenia: Why had Eve no fear of the measles?

Tammy: I can't guess.

Eugenia: She'd Adam.

❖ ❖ ❖

Eugenia: Why did the pig keep driving around the block?

Tammy: My mind is a blank.

Eugenia: He couldn't find a porking place.

❖ ❖ ❖

Eugenia: Why are rabbits never bald?
Tammy: I give up.
Eugenia: They're always raising hares.

❖ ❖ ❖

Eugenia: Why do people watch that quiz show?
Tammy: I don't know.
Eugenia: Me neither, it must be anybody's guess.

❖ ❖ ❖

Eugenia: Why did the dumb driver park at the intersection for two weeks?
Tammy: I'm a blank.
Eugenia: He was waiting for the stop sign to change to Go.

❖ ❖ ❖

Eugenia: Someone asked me why I don't drink tea anymore.
Tammy: What did you tell them?
Eugenia: I haven't liked it ever since that tea bag got stuck in my throat.

❖ ❖ ❖

Eugenia: Why does Santa's belly jiggle when he laughs?
Tammy: I pass.
Eugenia: 'Tis the season to be jelly.

11

School Daze

Teacher: When I was your age, Tommy, I could answer any question in arithmetic.
Tommy: Yes, but you had a different teacher than I had.

❖ ❖ ❖

Teacher: How can you tell the age of an elephant?
Class Clown: Count the candles on his birthday cake.

❖ ❖ ❖

Teacher: My hat will represent Mars.
Student: Is Mars inhabited?

❖ ❖ ❖

Teacher: Name the four food groups.
Student: Fast, canned, junk, and frozen.

❖ ❖ ❖

Teacher: What did the colonists wear at the Boston Tea Party?
Student: T-shirts?

❖ ❖ ❖

Teacher: (To student running in hall) Young man! What is your name? I'm going to report you to the principal.
Student: Marmaduke Ignatius Horatio Cornelius Fyvolentheimer, Junior.
Teacher: Well, just don't let me catch you again!

❖ ❖ ❖

Teacher: Can you name the Great Lakes?
Student: I don't need to. They've already been named.

❖ ❖ ❖

Teacher: This is the fifth day this week you had to stay after school. What have you got to say for yourself?
Student: Thank goodness it's Friday.

❖ ❖ ❖

Teacher: The law of gravitation explains why we stay on the ground.

Student: How did we stay on the ground before the law was passed?

❖ ❖ ❖

Teacher: Isn't it remarkable how fast trees grow?

Student: Not to me. They don't have anything else to do.

❖ ❖ ❖

Teacher: Why shouldn't you throw plastic bags into swamps in Louisiana?

Class Clown: The bags are not bayou degradable.

❖ ❖ ❖

Teacher: You can be sure that if Moses were alive today, he'd be considered a remarkable man.

Student: He sure would be. He'd be more than 2,500 years old!

❖ ❖ ❖

Gym Teacher: Do you know how to do a back flip?
Student: Is that a trick question?

12

Ashton & Audrey

Ashton: What do you call it when a kid can't go to school because he broke his leg playing soccer?

Audrey: I give up.

Ashton: A lame excuse.

❖ ❖ ❖

Ashton: What is the difference between Noah's Ark and an archbishop?

Audrey: I have no idea.

Ashton: One was a high ark, but the other is a hierarch.

❖ ❖ ❖

Ashton: What do you think of that new shopping program?
Audrey: I just can't buy it.

❖ ❖ ❖

Ashton: What did the monkey say when his sister had a baby?
Audrey: I don't have the foggiest.
Ashton: Well, I'll be a monkey's uncle!

❖ ❖ ❖

Ashton: What did the famous Indian fighter call his fast-food ice cream chain?
Audrey: You tell me.
Ashton: Custard's Last Stand.

❖ ❖ ❖

Ashton: What did the man say just before he glued his dog to the floor?
Audrey: I can't guess.
Ashton: Stickum, Fido!

❖ ❖ ❖

Ashton: What do lady polar bears put on their faces at night?
Audrey: My mind is a blank.
Ashton: Very cold cream.

❖ ❖ ❖

Ashton: What makes men bald?
Audrey: I give up.
Ashton: A lack of hair.

❖ ❖ ❖

Ashton: What does a waiter say if a skunk comes into his restaurant?
Audrey: That's a mystery.
Ashton: May I take your odor?

❖ ❖ ❖

Ashton: What do you call a man who has corns on his toes?
Audrey: I'm a blank.
Ashton: Paul Bunion.

❖ ❖ ❖

Ashton: What would you do if you were in my shoes?
Audrey: It's unknown to me.
Ashton: Shine them.

❖ ❖ ❖

Ashton: What letter travels the greatest distance?
Audrey: I'm in the dark.
Ashton: D, because it goes to the end of the world.

13

Bruce & Paul

Bruce: Why is Queen Elizabeth's son like photographs of large seagoing mammals?

Paul: I give up.

Bruce: They are both prints of whales.

❖ ❖ ❖

Bruce: Why were the stars of that new medical show fired?

Paul: I have no idea.

Bruce: They were all a bunch of cut-ups.

❖ ❖ ❖

Bruce: Why didn't they play cards on Noah's Ark?

Paul: Who knows?

Bruce: Noah sat on the deck.

❖ ❖ ❖

Bruce: Why did the cow take acting lessons?

Paul: I don't have the foggiest.

Bruce: He wanted to be a moo-vie star.

❖ ❖ ❖

Bruce: Did you hear about the youngster who asked his grandfather why he read his Bible all day long?

Paul: No, what was the grandfather's response?

Bruce: He said, "You might say I'm cramming for my final examinations."

❖ ❖ ❖

Bruce: I was asked why I watch so much soccer on TV.

Paul: What did you say?

Bruce: I get a kick out of it.

❖ ❖ ❖

Bruce: Why doesn't the Board of Health let bakeries sell orange juice?

Paul: My mind is a blank.

Bruce: Bakers can't be juicers.

❖ ❖ ❖

Bruce: Why is a good listener like a playful cat?
Paul: I give up.
Bruce: Both appreciate a good yarn.

❖ ❖ ❖

Bruce: Why did the geek throw his fishing line up into the air?
Paul: That's a mystery.
Bruce: He was fly fishing.

❖ ❖ ❖

Bruce: Why couldn't the bird speak?
Paul: I'm a blank.
Bruce: He had just paid the bill collector.

❖ ❖ ❖

Bruce: Why did the elephant have to give up jogging down the street?
Paul: It's unknown to me.
Bruce: He was causing potholes.

❖ ❖ ❖

Bruce: Why is the watermelon so full of water?
Paul: I'm in the dark.
Bruce: It's planted in the spring.

14

Did You Hear?

Did you hear about the weird man who was found dead in his jail cell with 12 bumps on his head?

He tried to hang himself with a rubber band.

❖ ❖ ❖

Did you hear about the man in New Zealand who found that a blood vessel on his wife's forehead enlarged with the decline of atmospheric pressure?

He began predicting with her weather vein.

❖ ❖ ❖

Did you hear about the country parson who decided to buy himself a horse?

The dealer assured him that the one he selected was a perfect choice. "This here horse," he said, "has lived all his life in a religious atmosphere. So remember that he'll never start if you order 'Giddyap.' You've got to say, 'Praise the Lord.' Likewise, a 'Whoa' will never make him stop. You've got to say, 'Amen.'"

Thus forewarned, the parson paid for the horse, mounted it, and with a cheery "Praise the Lord," headed toward his parish.

Suddenly, however, he noticed that the road ahead had been washed out, leaving a chasm 200 yards deep. In a panic, he yelled, "Whoa!" but the horse kept getting closer to the edge. The parson then yelled, "Stop!" but his horse continued to move ahead. Then he remembered the horse would stop only if the rider said amen. So he screamed, "Amen!" and the horse stopped right at the very edge of the cliff. The parson was shaking as he realized just how close he had come to falling down into the chasm. He was so overcome with joy and thankfulness he sighed, "Praise the Lord!"

❖ ❖ ❖

Did you hear about the dumb athlete who practiced his handwriting day and night so he'd have a chance of winning the pentathlon?

❖ ❖ ❖

1st boy: Did you drive in the nails?
2nd boy: No, I only have a learner's permit.

❖ ❖ ❖

Jack: Did you hear about the flood?
Mack: No, I didn't.
Jack: Oh, well. It's water under the bridge now.

❖ ❖ ❖

Rudy: Did you hear about the new cooking show?
Judy: It seemed a little overdone.

❖ ❖ ❖

Husband: Did you hear? Lamont's gettin' a Ph.D.
Wife: What does Ph.D. stand for?
Husband: In his case, Pin-headed Dope.

❖ ❖ ❖

Girl: Did you hear the story about the little wooden boy named Pinocchio?
Boy: No, what about him?
Girl: He got caught out in a rain storm and ended up with a warped mind.

❖ ❖ ❖

Did you hear that skunks never get rich? They just make a few scents.

❖ ❖ ❖

Did you hear that someone dropped a rubber band into the computer? Now it makes snap decisions.

❖ ❖ ❖

Did you hear that if you cross a carrier pigeon with a woodpecker you will get a bird that not only carries messages but will knock at the door when it arrives?

❖ ❖ ❖

Did you hear about the man who tried to buy a ticket for a trip to the moon? The travel agent told him all flights were canceled because the moon was full.

❖ ❖ ❖

Phyllis: Did you hear about the elephant who went to court?
Gillis: What happened to him?
Phyllis: Nothing. They couldn't build a case around him.

❖ ❖ ❖

Did you hear about the athlete who was so stupid that when he earned his varsity letter somebody had to read it to him?

❖ ❖ ❖

Did you hear about the Texan who moved to Oklahoma and raised the IQ level of both states?

❖ ❖ ❖

Mother: Did you hear me ask you to take out the garbage?
Son: Yes, but it already had a date.

15

Figaro & Rubrick

Figaro: Your name should be Algebra.
Rubrick: Why?
Figaro: I can't figure you out.

❖ ❖ ❖

Figaro: Did you hear about the castle ditch digger who fell asleep on the job?
Rubrick: No, what happened?
Figaro: He was de-moated.

❖ ❖ ❖

Figaro: Did you hear about the son who tried to explain to his mom why he was flying his model airplane in the backyard on Sunday?
Rubrick: No, what did he tell her?

Figaro: It was a missionary plane going to the jungle.

❖ ❖ ❖

Figaro (the customer): Excuse me, do you have any loafers?
Rubrick (the salesman): As a matter of fact, we do.
Figaro (the customer): Well, could you get one to wait on me?

❖ ❖ ❖

Figaro: If your brother gave you one dollar Monday and two dollars Tuesday, what would you have?
Rubrick: You tell me.
Figaro: A heart attack.

❖ ❖ ❖

Figaro: Did you hear about the boss who told his employee that if he couldn't keep up with his work he would have to get another clerk?
Rubrick: No, what happened?
Figaro: The clerk said, "Great! I could use some help."

❖ ❖ ❖

Figaro: Is it easy to click your fingers together?

Rubrick: I don't know.
Figaro: Sure. It's a snap.

❖ ❖ ❖

Figaro: My wife asked me if she made the toast too dark.
Rubrick: What did you say?
Figaro: I told her I couldn't tell. The smoke was too thick.

❖ ❖ ❖

Figaro: I named my racehorse Radish.
Rubrick: Why did you name him that?
Figaro: So when I see him, I can yell, "Here comes my horse, Radish."

❖ ❖ ❖

Figaro: Bet I can lift an elephant with six fingers.
Rubrick: Prove it.
Figaro: Show me an elephant with six fingers and I'll be glad to lift it.

❖ ❖ ❖

Figaro: Don't you think the new gardening show is great?
Rubrick: I guess so.
Figaro: Yeah, I think it really grows on you.

❖ ❖ ❖

Figaro: My friend who works in the oil fields came to the party all covered with petroleum.

Rubrick: What happened?

Figaro: Everyone exclaimed, "How crude!"

❖ ❖ ❖

Figaro: Some guy asked me if we had heavy rain here yesterday.

Rubrick: What did you tell him?

Figaro: I told him I didn't know because I didn't weigh it.

❖ ❖ ❖

Figaro: Which came first, the chicken or the egg?

Rubrick: You've got me guessing.

Figaro: The chicken, of course. God doesn't lay eggs.

16

Lisa & Lenny

Lisa: How long can a 3000-pound canary sing?
Lenny: I give up.
Lisa: As long as it wants.

❖ ❖ ❖

Lisa: How do you punish an eye doctor?
Lenny: I have no idea.
Lisa: Give him 40 lashes.

❖ ❖ ❖

Lisa: How can you tell if you're allergic to bees?
Lenny: Who knows?
Lisa: You'll break out in hives every time you see one.

❖ ❖ ❖

Lisa: How do you make an artichoke?
Lenny: I don't have the foggiest.
Lisa: Strangle it.

❖ ❖ ❖

Lisa: How did the crow cross the river?
Lenny: You tell me.
Lisa: In a crow boat.

❖ ❖ ❖

Lisa: How did they catch the gangster who committed the robbery on Mount Everest?
Lenny: I can't guess.
Lisa: He returned to the scene of the climb.

❖ ❖ ❖

Lisa: How long a period of time did Cain hate his brother?
Lenny: My mind is a blank.
Lisa: As long as he was Abel.

❖ ❖ ❖

Lisa: Did you hear about the pastor who asked the new church librarian how she liked her job?
Lenny: No, what happened?

Lisa: She told the pastor it was all right as long as people called her a librarian and not a bookie.

❖ ❖ ❖

Lisa: One of my friends asked me how I liked the new gardening show.
Lenny: What did you say?
Lisa: I told her I could take it or leaf it.

❖ ❖ ❖

Lisa: How many dumb players does it take to shoot a basketball?
Lenny: I'm a blank.
Lisa: Two. One to throw the ball and the other to fire the shotgun.

❖ ❖ ❖

Lisa: How does a weird artist paint a masterpiece?
Lenny: It's unknown to me.
Lisa: He just follows the numbers.

❖ ❖ ❖

Lisa: How do they prevent crime at McDonald's?
Lenny: I'm in the dark.
Lisa: With a burger alarm!

❖ ❖ ❖

Lisa: I had a guy ask me how I liked the new travel show.

Lenny: What did you say?

Lisa: I told him I thought it was really going places.

17

Penelope & Pollyanna

Penelope: My little sister asked me what I thought of the new game show on TV.
Pollyanna: What did you say?
Penelope: How many seconds do I have to answer?

❖ ❖ ❖

Penelope: What did the little turtles say to their teacher?
Pollyanna: I have no idea.
Penelope: You tortoise everything we know!

❖ ❖ ❖

Penelope: What word has six *I*'s?
Pollyanna: I don't have the foggiest.
Penelope: Indivisibility.

❖ ❖ ❖

Penelope: My mom asked me what I thought of the new medical show.

Pollyanna: What did you tell her?

Penelope: I told her I thought the script needed a lot of doctoring.

❖ ❖ ❖

Penelope: What do you call a candle named Lee?

Pollyanna: I can't guess.

Penelope: Wickedly.

❖ ❖ ❖

Penelope: What's the difference between a body builder and someone who's about to dig into a plate of clams?

Pollyanna: My mind is a blank.

Penelope: One's muscle-bound, the other mussel bound.

❖ ❖ ❖

Penelope: What did Adam say when Eve fell off the roof?

Pollyanna: I give up.

Penelope: Eve's dropping again!

❖ ❖ ❖

Penelope: What would you get if you crossed an elephant with a chicken?
Pollyanna: That's a mystery.
Penelope: The biggest coward in town.

❖ ❖ ❖

Penelope: What does Santa Claus say just before he tells a joke?
Pollyanna: I'm a blank.
Penelope: This'll sleigh you.

❖ ❖ ❖

Penelope: What do you get if you cross a toad and a pig?
Pollyanna: It's unknown to me.
Penelope: A wart hog.

❖ ❖ ❖

Penelope: What is a pig's favorite ballet?
Pollyanna: I'm in the dark.
Penelope: "Swine Lake."

❖ ❖ ❖

Penelope: What goes to college and carries lots of food?
Pollyanna: I pass.
Penelope: The Lunchbag of Notre Dame.

18

My, My, My

Floyd: My dog is smart.
Griff: How do you know?
Floyd: I asked him how much two minus two is and he said nothing.

❖ ❖ ❖

Floyd: My lawyer got hurt.
Griff: How did he get hurt?
Floyd: The ambulance backed up suddenly.

❖ ❖ ❖

Floyd: My new baby sister is cute as a button.
Griff: What's so cute about her?
Floyd: She has a round head with four holes in the middle.

❖ ❖ ❖

Floyd: My little brother told me his favorite TV show is "Lost in Space."

Griff: Do you agree with him?

Floyd: No. I told him I thought that was his state of mind.

❖ ❖ ❖

Floyd: My next door neighbor came over bragging that his dad had a sword of Washington and a hat of Lincoln.

Griff: What did you say?

Floyd: I told him my father has an Adam's apple.

❖ ❖ ❖

Floyd: My new assistant is from Hamburg, Germany.

Griff: So, what's wrong with that?

Floyd: Everyone keeps calling him my Hamburger helper.

❖ ❖ ❖

Floyd: My Indian friend said that his ancestors could dance and make it rain.

Griff: What did you say?

Floyd: I told him that was nothing because my parents could talk up a storm.

❖ ❖ ❖

Floyd: My uncle can shoot a gun faster than any other man in the West. He can even shoot without removing the gun from his holster.

Griff: What do they call your uncle?

Floyd: Three Toes Bill.

❖ ❖ ❖

Floyd: My girlfriend said her pastor is so good he can talk on any subject for an hour.

Griff: What was your response?

Floyd: I told her that was nothing because my pastor can talk for an hour without a subject.

❖ ❖ ❖

Floyd: My dad is so absent-minded instead of cornflakes he gave me soapflakes for breakfast.

Griff: I bet that made you mad.

Floyd: Mad? I was foaming at the mouth.

❖ ❖ ❖

Floyd: My oldest brother, the magician, is going to saw my youngest brother in half.

Griff: So what does that make your youngest brother?

Floyd: That makes him my half-brother.

❖ ❖ ❖

Floyd: My report card went from B's to D's.
Griff: How terrible.
Floyd: Yeah, pretty degrading!

❖ ❖ ❖

Floyd: My friend told me his TV set was on the blink.
Griff: That's too bad.
Floyd: Yeah, I told him mine's on a little stand.

19

Jon-Mark & Walter

Jon-Mark: How many judges does it take to change a light bulb?

Walter: I give up.

Jon-Mark: Two. One to turn it and one to overturn it.

❖ ❖ ❖

Jon-Mark: How does a robot keep from losing its temper?

Walter: I have no idea.

Jon-Mark: It counts to tin first.

❖ ❖ ❖

Jon-Mark: How did ducks get flat feet?

Walter: Who knows?

Jon-Mark: Teaching clumsy elephants how to waltz.

❖ ❖ ❖

Jon-Mark: How do you stop a cup from leaking?

Walter: I don't have the foggiest.

Jon-Mark: Empty it.

❖ ❖ ❖

Jon-Mark: How do you like school?

Walter: You tell me.

Jon-Mark: Closed.

❖ ❖ ❖

Jon-Mark: How do you know money talks?

Walter: I can't guess.

Jon-Mark: I'm making every cent count.

❖ ❖ ❖

Jon-Mark: How do we know they used arithmetic in early Bible times?

Walter: My mind is a blank.

Jon-Mark: The Lord said to multiply on the face of the earth.

❖ ❖ ❖

Jon-Mark: Some guy asked me how I felt about smog.
Walter: What did you say?
Jon-Mark: I told him I always get choked up about it.

❖ ❖ ❖

Jon-Mark: How does a cobbler chase away a fly?
Walter: That's a mystery.
Jon-Mark: He shoos it.

❖ ❖ ❖

Jon-Mark: How do most lawyers buy food?
Walter: I'm a blank.
Jon-Mark: By the case!

❖ ❖ ❖

Jon-Mark: How can a submarine tell if it's in France or not?
Walter: It's unknown to me.
Jon-Mark: By using its Paris-scope.

❖ ❖ ❖

Jon-Mark: How is life like a doughnut?
Walter: I'm in the dark.
Jon-Mark: You are either in the dough or in the hole.

❖ ❖ ❖

Jon-Mark: How do camels hide in the desert?
Walter: I pass.
Jon-Mark: They wear camel-flage.

20

Bertram & Bunsby

Bertram: Did you hear about the father who asked his son if he had heard the story about his forebears?

Bunsby: No, what happened?

Bertram: The little boy told him he hadn't heard that story but he'd heard the one about the three bears.

❖ ❖ ❖

Bertram: Your name should be Laryngitis.

Bunsby: Why?

Bertram: You're a pain in the neck.

❖ ❖ ❖

Bertram: You're not very smart!

Bunsby: Don't I go to school, stupid?
Bertram: Yes, and you come home the same way!

❖ ❖ ❖

Bertram: My little brother says he does great impersonations.
Bunsby: Did you have him do any?
Bertram: Yes. I told him to impersonate Houdini and make himself disappear.

❖ ❖ ❖

Bertram: Did you hear the story about when Eve asked Adam "Do you love me?"
Bunsby: No, what did he say?
Bertram: He said, "Who else?"

❖ ❖ ❖

Bertram: Was there any money on Noah's Ark?
Bunsby: I don't know.
Bertram: Yes. The duck took a bill, the frog took a greenback, and the skunk took a scent.

❖ ❖ ❖

Bertram: Did you hear about the guy who was being accused of stealing garments from the clothesline of a convent?

Bunsby: No, what happened?
Bertram: He promised he wouldn't make a habit of it.

❖ ❖ ❖

Bertram: Your smile reminds me of a movie star.
Bunsby: Really? Which one?
Bertram: Popeye. There's spinach between your teeth.

❖ ❖ ❖

Bertram: In what place did the cock crow when all the world could hear him?
Bunsby: That's a mystery.
Bertram: In Noah's Ark.

❖ ❖ ❖

Bertram: Playing golf must be bad for your heart.
Bunsby: What makes you say that?
Bertram: I just heard a golfer say he had four strokes on the very first hole.

❖ ❖ ❖

Bertram: Have you ever seen a tree move?
Bunsby: No, never.

Bertram: Then you probably haven't seen a walking stick.

❖ ❖ ❖

Bertram: In what jungle do you find pigmies?
Bunsby: I'm in the dark.
Bertram: In the Hamazon.

❖ ❖ ❖

Bertram: If fruit comes from a fruit tree, what kind of tree does a chicken come from?
Bunsby: You've got me guessing.
Bertram: A poul-tree!

❖ ❖ ❖

Bertram: Which animal is the best athlete?
Bunsby: How should I know?
Bertram: The bowler bear.

21

Daffy Definitions

Abdomen: Men from the invisible planet Abdo.

❖ ❖ ❖

Acoustic: The instrument used in shooting pool.

❖ ❖ ❖

Aftermath: The period following algebra.

❖ ❖ ❖

Air Traffic Control: Your teacher confiscating your paper airplane.

❖ ❖ ❖

American: A person who yells for the government to balance the budget and then borrows five dollars till payday.

❖ ❖ ❖

Antipollution Rally: What your parents hold every time they look under your bed.

❖ ❖ ❖

Astronomer: A night watchman.

❖ ❖ ❖

Baby-sitter: A teenage girl you hire to let your children do whatever they want.

❖ ❖ ❖

Barium: What you do with dead people.

❖ ❖ ❖

Big Dipper: Someone you don't want to get stuck behind at an all-you-can-eat buffet.

❖ ❖ ❖

Bone Voyage: A wife saying goodbye to her anthropologist husband as he leaves for an expedition.

❖ ❖ ❖

Boron: What a teacher shouldn't be.

❖ ❖ ❖

Coincide: What you should do when it's raining.

❖ ❖ ❖

Cold Front: What you get when you stare into the refrigerator too long.

❖ ❖ ❖

Cold Spell: A spelling bee in Alaska.

❖ ❖ ❖

Declared a Disaster Area: What the school principal did to your locker.

❖ ❖ ❖

Early Morning Mist: Walking into the bathroom while your sister's spraying her hair.

❖ ❖ ❖

Earthquake: A topographical error.

❖ ❖ ❖

Economic Slowdown: A cut in your weekly allowance.

❖ ❖ ❖

Flash Flood: What happens when your water balloon suddenly bursts.

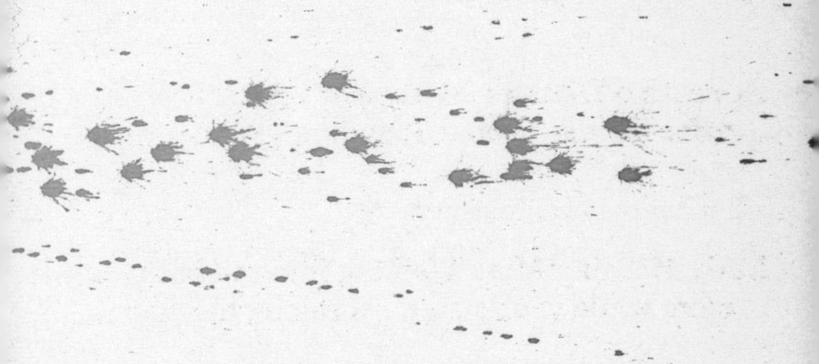

22

Christy & Julie

Christy: How did Jill fix her flat tire?
Julie: I give up.
Christy: With her Jack.

❖ ❖ ❖

Christy: How does an Indian know what's on television?
Julie: I have no idea.
Christy: He looks it up in the Teepee Guide.

❖ ❖ ❖

Christy: How does a stupid weightlifter get a dumbbell into the air?
Julie: Who knows?
Christy: He jumps!

❖ ❖ ❖

Christy: How can you be sure to start a fire with two sticks?
Julie: I don't have the foggiest.
Christy: Make sure one of them is a match.

❖ ❖ ❖

Christy: How were Adam and Eve prevented from gambling?
Julie: You tell me.
Christy: Their pair-of-dice was taken away from them.

❖ ❖ ❖

Christy: How were the hamburgers taken to the police station?
Julie: I can't guess.
Christy: In a patty wagon.

❖ ❖ ❖

Christy: How does the butcher speak?
Julie: My mind is a blank.
Christy: He talks turkey.

❖ ❖ ❖

Christy: How is a horse like a bartender?
Julie: I give up.

Christy: It gives its bit and listens to every woe.

❖ ❖ ❖

Christy: How does a weird person make hot water?

Julie: That's a mystery.

Christy: He microwaves an ice cube.

❖ ❖ ❖

Christy: My mom asked me if I like the new educational history program.

Julie: What did you tell her?

Christy: It doesn't cover anything new.

❖ ❖ ❖

Christy: How can you tell if a postcard is from Mars?

Julie: It's unknown to me.

Christy: It's from Mars if there's space between the lines.

❖ ❖ ❖

Christy: How do you warm up a room after it's been painted?

Julie: I'm in the dark.

Christy: Give it a second coat.

❖ ❖ ❖

Christy: Did you hear about the little corn who asked the mother corn how he got here? The mother corn told him that the stalk brought him.

Julie: What did the little corn say after hearing her answer?

Christy: He said, "You mean there's no Popcorn?"

23

Carmen & Cordelia

Carmen: What is yellow and ducks in and out of traffic?

Cordelia: I give up.

Carmen: A jaywalking banana.

❖ ❖ ❖

Carmen: What would you call an eagle who could play the piano with its feet?

Cordelia: I have no idea.

Carmen: Very talon-ted.

❖ ❖ ❖

Carmen: What five-letter word of three letters has six left after you take two away?

Cordelia: Who knows?
Carmen: S-i-x-t-y.

❖ ❖ ❖

Carmen: What is a cow's favorite Olympic event?
Cordelia: I don't have the foggiest.
Carmen: The hurdles.

❖ ❖ ❖

Carmen: What do you think about that police show getting canceled?
Cordelia: I think it's a bummer.
Carmen: Yeah, it's a crime.

❖ ❖ ❖

Carmen: What do you get when you cross a court show with a gardening show?
Cordelia: You tell me.
Carmen: A lot of buried facts.

❖ ❖ ❖

Carmen: What is a reptile's favorite movie?
Cordelia: I can't guess.
Carmen: The Lizard of Oz.

❖ ❖ ❖

Carmen: What do you get when you put a giant fish in your living room?
Cordelia: My mind is a blank.
Carmen: Whale-to-whale carpeting.

❖ ❖ ❖

Carmen: What do baby snakes play with?
Cordelia: I give up.
Carmen: Rattlers.

❖ ❖ ❖

Carmen: What TV cowboy wears a mask, has a friend just like Tonto, and rides a horse just like Silver?
Cordelia: That's a mystery.
Carmen: The Clone Ranger.

❖ ❖ ❖

Carmen: What do you call a very small rodent?
Cordelia: I'm a blank.
Carmen: A mini-mouse.

❖ ❖ ❖

Carmen: What kind of games do Texas ranch hands play while riding around in their cars?
Cordelia: It's unknown to me.
Carmen: Cowboys and Engines.

24

Ryan & Danny

Ryan: Who was the chubbiest ruler of Egypt?
Danny: I give up.
Ryan: Cleofatra.

❖ ❖ ❖

Ryan: Who was the most popular actor in the Bible?
Danny: I have no idea.
Ryan: Samson. He brought the house down.

❖ ❖ ❖

Ryan: Who introduced the first walking stick?
Danny: Who knows?
Ryan: Eve—when she presented Adam a little Cain.

❖ ❖ ❖

Ryan: Who was the clumsiest nursery rhyme character?

Danny: I don't have the foggiest.

Ryan: Little Miss Muff-It.

❖ ❖ ❖

Ryan: Who rides a white horse, wears a mask, and is desperate for company?

Danny: You tell me.

Ryan: The Lonely Ranger.

❖ ❖ ❖

Ryan: Who was the most successful physician in the Bible?

Danny: I can't guess.

Ryan: Job—he had the most patience.

❖ ❖ ❖

Ryan: Who was the straightest man in the Bible?

Danny: My mind is a blank.

Ryan: Joseph. Pharaoh made a ruler out of him.

❖ ❖ ❖

Ryan: Who sounded the first bell in the Bible?

Danny: I give up.

Ryan: Cain, when he hit Abel.

❖ ❖ ❖

Ryan: Who was the fastest runner in the world?
Danny: That's a mystery.
Ryan: Adam—he was first in the human race.

❖ ❖ ❖

Ryan: Who succeeded the first president?
Danny: I'm a blank.
Ryan: The second one.

❖ ❖ ❖

Ryan: Who helped the beautiful fish go to the underwater ball?
Danny: It's unknown to me.
Ryan: Her fairy cod-mother.

❖ ❖ ❖

Ryan: Who is the smallest man in the Bible?
Danny: I'm in the dark.
Ryan: Some people believe that it was Zacchaeus. Others believe it was Bildad, the Shuhite. But in reality it was Peter, the disciple—he slept on his watch!

❖ ❖ ❖

Ryan: Who was the meanest chicken that ever lived?
Danny: I pass.
Ryan: Attila the Hen.

❖ ❖ ❖

Ryan: Who would you find living with seven fat dwarfs?
Danny: You've got me guessing.
Ryan: Snow Wide.

❖ ❖ ❖

Ryan: Who is the patron saint of barbers who gives shaves?
Danny: How should I know?
Ryan: St. Nickolaus.

❖ ❖ ❖

Ryan: Who sits on top of cakes in the winter-time?
Danny: Search me.
Ryan: Frosting, the Snowman.

25

Questions & Answers

When was money first mentioned in the Bible?

When the dove brought the green back to the ark.

❖ ❖ ❖

When is a sick man a contradiction?

When he is an impatient patient.

❖ ❖ ❖

When Washington crossed the Delaware, what did he see on his left hand?

He saw five fingers.

❖ ❖ ❖

When does a farmer need a plumber?
When there are leeks in his garden.

❖ ❖ ❖

When is a tree frightened?
When it's petrified.

❖ ❖ ❖

When is the only time a fisherman tells the truth?
When he calls another fisherman a liar.

❖ ❖ ❖

When you have 50 people all of different opinions, what do you have?
A Baptist church.

❖ ❖ ❖

When did Moses sleep with five people in one bed?
When he slept with his forefathers.

❖ ❖ ❖

When does a fireplace change shape?
When smoke curls up the chimney.

❖ ❖ ❖

Why does your dog walk in circles before going to bed?

He's a watchdog and he's winding himself up.

❖ ❖ ❖

When should the letter "V" go into a room?

After "U."

❖ ❖ ❖

Who should you eat out with—Rick or Nick?

When you are going to eat, always pick Nick.

❖ ❖ ❖

When do all-beef hamburgers enjoy watching TV the most?

During prime time.

❖ ❖ ❖

When do people who yell a lot celebrate?

On holler-days.

❖ ❖ ❖

When a librarian goes fishing, what does she use for bait?

Bookworms.

❖ ❖ ❖

Why did the moron put warm bread in the blender?

So he could drink a toast.

26

Ajax & Ali-Baba

Ajax: My mother told me to answer the phone.
Ali-baba: Well, did you?
Ajax: I told her I hadn't heard its question yet.

❖ ❖ ❖

Ajax: I think I know why they call them soap operas.
Ali-baba: Why is that?
Ajax: My sister always works herself up into a lather over them.

❖ ❖ ❖

Ajax: Sometimes I get so depressed I want to drown myself.
Ali-baba: What stops you?
Ajax: I can't swim.

❖ ❖ ❖

Ajax: Did you hear about the customer who asked the waiter if his chef had chicken legs?

Ali-baba: No, what happened?

Ajax: The waiter said he didn't know because he couldn't see under his apron.

❖ ❖ ❖

Ajax: Have you heard of the new drive-in confessional?

Ali-baba: No, what's it called?

Ajax: Toot and Tell.

❖ ❖ ❖

Ajax: Did you hear about the customer who told his waiter that the spicy food was giving him heartburn?

Ali-baba: No, what happened?

Ajax: The waiter said, "What did you expect—sunburn?"

❖ ❖ ❖

Ajax: Which league plays baseball with coal instead of with a hardball?

Ali-baba: My mind is a blank.

Ajax: The miner league.

❖ ❖ ❖

Ajax: Last night my computer died.
Ali-baba: What did it die of?
Ajax: A terminal illness.

❖ ❖ ❖

Ajax: Did you hear about the cowboy who told his Indian friend that he broke three wild horses?
Ali-baba: No, what did his friend say?
Ajax: How careless of you!

❖ ❖ ❖

Ajax: Don't you think Buck Rogers' wife is a nice lady?
Ali-baba: She's okay.
Ajax: Well, I think she's a little deer.

❖ ❖ ❖

Ajax: At what time of day was Adam born?
Ali-baba: It's unknown to me.
Ajax: A little before Eve.

❖ ❖ ❖

Ajax: Why was Moses the most wicked man who ever lived?
Ali-baba: I'm in the dark.

Ajax: He broke ten commandments all at once.

❖ ❖ ❖

Ajax: Have you ever been in an earthquake?
Ali-baba: No, have you?
Ajax: Can't sway that I have.

❖ ❖ ❖

Ajax: My friend asked me if I wanted to see him rope a mule.
Ali-baba: What did you say?
Ajax: I told him I was tied up at the moment.

❖ ❖ ❖

Ajax: If a man who is carrying a dozen glass lamps drops one, what does he become?
Ali-baba: How should I know?
Ajax: A lamp lighter.

27

Pam & Melba

Pam: How do you help an alligator?
Melba: I give up.
Pam: With Gator Aid.

❖ ❖ ❖

Pam: How do you clear ice off the windows of tall buildings?
Melba: I have no idea.
Pam: With a sky scraper.

❖ ❖ ❖

Pam: How did Mary's little lamb go to the moon?
Melba: Who knows?
Pam: By rocket sheep.

❖ ❖ ❖

Pam: How did ten dumb climbers fall off the cliff?
Melba: I don't have the foggiest.
Pam: Playing follow-the-leader.

❖ ❖ ❖

Pam: How did Jonah feel when the great fish swallowed him?
Melba: You tell me.
Pam: Down in the mouth.

❖ ❖ ❖

Pam: How does a weird man dial 911?
Melba: I can't guess.
Pam: First he calls the operator and asks for the number.

❖ ❖ ❖

Pam: How do trees fight?
Melba: My mind is a blank.
Pam: They have a tree-for-all.

❖ ❖ ❖

Pam: I told my husband that I wanted to watch the new travel show tonight?
Melba: What did he say?
Pam: Get out of town!

❖ ❖ ❖

Pam: How did the weird boy finally make his mark in school?
Melba: That's a mystery.
Pam: He wrote on the walls.

❖ ❖ ❖

Pam: How did the tiger become a star?
Melba: I'm a blank.
Pam: He clawed his way to the top.

❖ ❖ ❖

Pam: How big is the average American's foot?
Melba: It's unknown to me.
Pam: Exactly 12 inches.

❖ ❖ ❖

Pam: How many rocks should a thirsty man collect?
Melba: I'm in the dark.
Pam: About two quartz.

28

Emile & Elmo

Emile: What do you call the mate of a male mouse?

Elmo: I give up.

Emile: A mousewife.

❖ ❖ ❖

Emile: What's the difference between a boxer and a man with a cold?

Elmo: I have no idea.

Emile: One knows his blows, the other blows his nose.

❖ ❖ ❖

Emile: What kinds of jokes do vegetables like best?

Elmo: Who knows?

Emile: Corny ones!

❖ ❖ ❖

Emile: What is long and skinny and flies?

Elmo: I don't have the foggiest.

Emile: Super-spaghetti.

❖ ❖ ❖

Emile: What do they call a tennis player's income?

Elmo: You tell me.

Emile: Net earnings.

❖ ❖ ❖

Emile: What is a candle's favorite part of the week?

Elmo: I can't guess.

Emile: The wick-end.

❖ ❖ ❖

Emile: What do you call a broken mountaineering pick?

Elmo: My mind is a blank.

Emile: An anti-climb ax.

❖ ❖ ❖

Emile: What army officer works in the coal fields?
Elmo: I give up.
Emile: The major miner.

❖ ❖ ❖

Emile: What kind of fish can't keep a secret?
Elmo: That's a mystery.
Emile: A big-mouth bass.

❖ ❖ ❖

Emile: What game do strange mothers play with their babies?
Elmo: I'm a blank.
Emile: Geekaboo!

❖ ❖ ❖

Emile: What's the main qualification for having a military funeral?
Elmo: It's unknown to me.
Emile: You must be dead.

❖ ❖ ❖

Emile: What do monsters play at parties?
Elmo: I'm in the dark.
Emile: Hide and freak.

❖ ❖ ❖

Emile: What kind of storm moves the fastest?
Elmo: I pass.
Emile: A hurry-cane.

29

Stop That Knocking!

Knock, knock.
Who's there?
Annette.
Annette who?
Annette is what you need to play tennis.

❖ ❖ ❖

Knock, knock.
Who's there?
Eileen.
Eileen who?
Eileen down to tie my shoelaces.

❖ ❖ ❖

Knock, knock.
Who's there?

Isle.
Isle who?
Isle give you a big kiss if you open the door.

❖ ❖ ❖

Knock, knock.
Who's there?
Nod.
Nod who?
Nod you again!

❖ ❖ ❖

Knock, knock.
Who's there?
Water.
Water who?
Water you know.

❖ ❖ ❖

Knock, knock.
Who's there?
Eiffel.
Eiffel who?
Eiffel down and broke my crown.

❖ ❖ ❖

Knock, knock.
Who's there?

Turnip.
Turnip who?
Turnip the TV.

❖ ❖ ❖

Knock, knock.
Who's there?
C-I-A.
C-I-A who?
C-I-Ate the whole cake!

❖ ❖ ❖

Knock, knock.
Who's there?
Wendy.
Wendy who?
Wendy red, red robin comes bob, bob, bobbin' along.

❖ ❖ ❖

Knock, knock.
Who's there?
Sanctuary.
Sanctuary who?
Sanctuary much!
You're welcome!

❖ ❖ ❖

Knock, knock.
Who's there?
Annapolis.
Annapolis who?
Ann-apol-is a fruit.

❖ ❖ ❖

Knock, knock.
Who's there?
I, Sherwood.
I, Sherwood who?
I, Sherwood like to go home early from school today.

30

Don & Mike

Don: My older brother asked me if I wanted to watch a scary movie tonight.
Mike: What did you say?
Don: I'm afraid not!

❖ ❖ ❖

Don: My wife asked me if I thought there were too many shootings in westerns.
Mike: What did you say?
Don: That's a loaded question.

❖ ❖ ❖

Don: I asked my sister if she liked that new horror show.
Mike: Well, did she?
Don: Yea, she said it was a scream.

❖ ❖ ❖

Don: I didn't like that new animal show.
Mike: Why not?
Don: I thought it was a dog.

❖ ❖ ❖

Don: My wife asked me if I thought television encouraged violent behavior.
Mike: What did you tell her?
Don: I told her only if she tries to change my channel.

❖ ❖ ❖

Don: My little brother asked me if I thought it were possible to communicate with the dead.
Mike: What did you say?
Don: He was certainly coming in loud and clear.

❖ ❖ ❖

Don: My friend asked me if I thought we should continue to explore outer space.
Mike: What did you tell him?
Don: Of course. I told him he was entitled to learn about his birthplace.

❖ ❖ ❖

Don: Do you know much about gophers?

Mike: Not really.

Don: Me neither. I don't know a gopher from a mole in the ground.

❖ ❖ ❖

Don: My girlfriend asked me if I liked to watch shows about poisonous snakes.

Mike: What was your answer?

Don: No, they get me rattled.

❖ ❖ ❖

Don: Do you exercise daily?

Mike: No, do you?

Don: No, Daily can exercise himself.

❖ ❖ ❖

Don: Do you believe in letting sleeping dogs lie?

Mike: Yes, do you?

Don: No, they should tell the truth.

❖ ❖ ❖

Don: Do you know how you can tell that David was older than Goliath?

Mike: No, how can you tell?

Don: David rocked Goliath to sleep.

❖ ❖ ❖

Don: Do you think leopards have keen eyesight?

Mike: I don't know, what do you think?

Don: Yes. They can spot things from miles away.

❖ ❖ ❖

Don: Do you like the new detective show?

Mike: Not really, what about you?

Don: I'll need to investigate it further.

❖ ❖ ❖

Don: I asked my mom if she liked sad movies.

Mike: What did she say?

Don: She said, "No, for crying out loud."

❖ ❖ ❖

Don: Do you like shows about fish?

Mike: No, do you?

Don: Yea, they really hook me.

❖ ❖ ❖

Don: Do you like that new cooking show?

Mike: Yea, I think it's great!

Don: Well, it's not my cup of tea.

❖ ❖ ❖

Don: Do fish perspire?
Mike: You got me.
Don: Of course, what do you think makes the sea so salty?

31

Filbert & Grundy

Filbert: What's the dumbest question to ask in an antique store?
Grundy: I give up.
Filbert: What's new?

❖ ❖ ❖

Filbert: What kind of sports cars do queen bees drive?
Grundy: I have no idea.
Filbert: Stingrays.

❖ ❖ ❖

Filbert: What kind of stories do rabbits tell?
Grundy: Who knows?
Filbert: Cotton-tales.

❖ ❖ ❖

Filbert: What kind of sand is always in a hurry?
Grundy: I don't have the foggiest.
Filbert: Quicksand.

❖ ❖ ❖

Filbert: What's written on the Christmas card sent out by the coach at Notre Dame?
Grundy: You tell me.
Filbert: Irish you a Merry Christmas.

❖ ❖ ❖

Filbert: What do you get when you cross an educational show with a comedy?
Grundy: I can't guess.
Filbert: A brain teaser.

❖ ❖ ❖

Filbert: What would you get if you crossed Kris Kringle with a bandage?
Grundy: My mind is a blank.
Filbert: Santa Gauze.

❖ ❖ ❖

Filbert: What is gray, has a trunk but no tags, and keeps circling the airport?

Grundy: I give up.
Filbert: An unclaimed elephant on the baggage carousel.

❖ ❖ ❖

Filbert: What newspaper do stockbrokers in Alaska read?
Grundy: That's a mystery.
Filbert: The Walrus Street Journal.

❖ ❖ ❖

Filbert: What do you call the owner of a flower shop when he can't move?
Grundy: I'm a blank.
Filbert: The petrified florist.

❖ ❖ ❖

Filbert: What does an auto mechanic charge to fix a tire?
Grundy: It's unknown to me.
Filbert: A flat rate.

❖ ❖ ❖

Filbert: What did the dumb man say when his house caught on fire?
Grundy: I'm in the dark.
Filbert: Gee, home cooking!

32

Royce & Heather

Royce: Why did the parakeet land on the fish's back?

Heather: I give up.

Royce: He was looking for a perch.

❖ ❖ ❖

Royce: Why don't grapes ever get lonely?

Heather: I have no idea.

Royce: They hang around in bunches.

❖ ❖ ❖

Royce: Why did the man seek employment in the dynamite factory?

Heather: Who knows?

Royce: He wanted a job that was a real blast.

❖ ❖ ❖

Royce: Why is number six afraid of number seven?
Heather: I don't have the foggiest.
Royce: Seven, eight, nine.

❖ ❖ ❖

Royce: Why was the weeping willow punished?
Heather: You tell me.
Royce: For crying out loud.

❖ ❖ ❖

Royce: Why are there so few men with whiskers in heaven?
Heather: I can't guess.
Royce: Most men get in by a close shave.

❖ ❖ ❖

Royce: Why is a confused man like the number 8?
Heather: My mind is a blank.
Royce: They both go around in circles.

❖ ❖ ❖

Royce: Why shouldn't you utter a secret in a bank?
Heather: I give up.
Royce: The place is full of tellers.

❖ ❖ ❖

Royce: Why did Mrs. Kangaroo leave her baby home when she went to the city?
Heather: That's a mystery.
Royce: She was afraid of pickpockets!

❖ ❖ ❖

Royce: Why did the weird man take a shower in his clothes?
Heather: I'm a blank.
Royce: The tag on them said Wash and Wear.

❖ ❖ ❖

Royce: Why should you always carry a deck of cards in your car?
Heather: It's unknown to me.
Royce: If you get a flat, you'll have four Jacks with you.

❖ ❖ ❖

Royce: Why was the nervous carpenter fired?
Heather: I'm in the dark.
Royce: He was constantly biting his nails.

❖ ❖ ❖

Royce: Why doesn't your parrot say what you tell him to?
Heather: I pass.
Royce: He believes in freedom of screech.

33

More Did You Hear?

Did you hear that Ben Franklin discovered electricity after his wife told him to go fly a kite?

❖ ❖ ❖

Did you hear that a diamond is one of the hardest things on earth . . . to get back?

❖ ❖ ❖

Did you hear about the redneck who planted Cheerios in his backyard? He thought they were donut seeds.

❖ ❖ ❖

Talk about a tough kid. All his tattooing is done by a stone mason.

❖ ❖ ❖

Did you hear about the man who invented rope and built a huge hempire?

❖ ❖ ❖

Did you hear the police finally caught that cat burglar? He was purr-owling the neighborhood.

❖ ❖ ❖

Did you hear about the nose-drop salesman who kept insisting people try his product? He was fired for sticking his business into other people's noses.

❖ ❖ ❖

Young Victor said to his older brother Chris, "Did you know that it takes longer to run from second to third than from third to home?"

Chris scratched his head. "How can that be?"

"There's a shortstop between them."

❖ ❖ ❖

Did you hear there's a new movie about a dentist who goes back and forth in time? It's called *Plaque to the Future.*

❖ ❖ ❖

Have you heard? The Three Little Pigs once did time in the pen.

❖ ❖ ❖

Did you hear I was the teacher's pet? She couldn't afford a dog.

❖ ❖ ❖

Did you hear about the baseball player who hit a foul? The bird didn't even complain.

❖ ❖ ❖

Did you hear about the Smogarian orchestra that stopped in the middle of a performance to clean the saliva out of their instruments? It just happened to be a string orchestra.

❖ ❖ ❖

Did the doctor give you first aid? No, I had to wait my turn.

34

Barkley & Beatrice

Barkley: What game do little weirdos like to play?

Beatrice: I give up.

Barkley: Hide-and-Geek.

❖ ❖ ❖

Barkley: What do hogs take when they have tired blood?

Beatrice: I have no idea.

Barkley: Pig iron.

❖ ❖ ❖

Barkley: What do ecologists eat for dessert?

Beatrice: Who knows?

Barkley: Environ-mints.

❖ ❖ ❖

Barkley: What is hairy, primitive, and goes "Oink, oink?"
Beatrice: I don't have the foggiest.
Barkley: The Missing Sausage Link.

❖ ❖ ❖

Barkley: What's the most important thing to have when ice fishing?
Beatrice: You tell me.
Barkley: Excellent ice site.

❖ ❖ ❖

Barkley: What has three feet and can't walk?
Beatrice: I can't guess.
Barkley: A yard.

❖ ❖ ❖

Barkley: What would you get if you crossed a doctor with a hyena?
Beatrice: My mind is a blank.
Barkley: A physician who laughs all the way to the bank.

❖ ❖ ❖

Barkley: What's the laziest mountain in the world?

Beatrice: I give up.
Barkley: Mt. Everest.

❖ ❖ ❖

Barkley: What did one hip say to the other hip?
Beatrice: That's a mystery.
Barkley: Thigh, neighbor!

❖ ❖ ❖

Barkley: What are the first sounds you hear when a clumsy man tries to juggle three eggs?
Beatrice: I'm a blank.
Barkley: Splat! Splat! Splat!

❖ ❖ ❖

Barkley: What did one match say to the other match?
Beatrice: It's unknown to me.
Barkley: I'm burned out.

❖ ❖ ❖

Barkley: What is the difference between a book of fiction and the rear light of a car?
Beatrice: I'm in the dark.
Barkley: One is a light tale, and the other is a tail light.

35

Brenda & Rich

Brenda: Why does a pitcher raise one leg when he winds up?

Rich: I give up.

Brenda: If he raised them both, he'd fall down.

❖ ❖ ❖

Brenda: What do hostesses insist on doing?

Rich: I have no idea.

Brenda: Introducing us to people we don't know.

❖ ❖ ❖

Brenda: Why couldn't the weird boy open his school locker?

Rich: Who knows?

Brenda: He didn't have a key to his combination lock.

❖ ❖ ❖

Brenda: Why are rivers rich?

Rich: I don't have the foggiest.

Brenda: Every river has two banks.

❖ ❖ ❖

Brenda: Why did the farmer buy so much land?

Rich: I'm a blank.

Brenda: He got it dirt cheap.

❖ ❖ ❖

Brenda: Why was Job always cold in bed?

Rich: It's unknown to me.

Brenda: He had such miserable comforters.

❖ ❖ ❖

Brenda: Why did the basketball player wear a bib?

Rich: I'm in the dark.

Brenda: He dribbled so much.

❖ ❖ ❖

Brenda: Why does an Indian wear a headdress?
Rich: I pass.
Brenda: To keep his wigwam.

❖ ❖ ❖

Brenda: Why do you think football is such a rough sport?
Rich: You've got me guessing.
Brenda: That's a tough question to tackle.

❖ ❖ ❖

Brenda: Why was the oyster mad at the clam?
Rich: How should I know?
Brenda: The clam was being shellfish.

❖ ❖ ❖

Brenda: Why should you call someone who is 11 inches tall "prince?"
Rich: Search me.
Brenda: At 12 inches, he'll become a ruler.

❖ ❖ ❖

Brenda: Why wouldn't the man buy a jigsaw puzzle?
Rich: I have no clue.
Brenda: He didn't want any part of it.

❖ ❖ ❖

Brenda: Why didn't the lake like the pond?
Rich: I don't know.
Brenda: The lake thought the pond was very shallow.

36

Jerome & Oswald

Jerome: What do you call a person who gives a candle a hug?
Oswald: I give up.
Jerome: A candle holder.

❖ ❖ ❖

Jerome: What is the opposite of meteorite?
Oswald: I have no idea.
Jerome: Meteorleft or meteorwrong.

❖ ❖ ❖

Jerome: What do you think about that new educational show?
Oswald: Who knows?
Jerome: It doesn't make the grade.

❖ ❖ ❖

Jerome: What's the difference between a sewage plant and a sit-up?
Oswald: I don't have the foggiest.
Jerome: One is good for waste treatment, the other's good for treating your waist.

❖ ❖ ❖

Jerome: What do you get when two pickles bump into each other?
Oswald: You tell me.
Jerome: A pickle jar.

❖ ❖ ❖

Jerome: What is red and yawns?
Oswald: I can't guess.
Jerome: A tomato with insomnia.

❖ ❖ ❖

Jerome: What do you think of that new police show?
Oswald: My mind is a blank.
Jerome: I think it's just the ticket.

❖ ❖ ❖

Jerome: What would you use to cut an ocean in two?

Oswald: I give up.

Jerome: A see-saw.

❖ ❖ ❖

Jerome: What is the most common educational problem in Smogaria?

Oswald: That's a mystery.

Jerome: Kindergarten dropout.

❖ ❖ ❖

Jerome: What's the difference between a doctor and a specialist?

Oswald: I'm a blank.

Jerome: About two weeks' pay.

❖ ❖ ❖

Jerome: What do you get if you cross a pig with a frog?

Oswald: It's unknown to me.

Jerome: A hamphibian.

❖ ❖ ❖

Jerome: What animals are the most reckless gamblers?

Oswald: I'm in the dark.

Jerome: Cows. They play for big steaks.

❖ ❖ ❖

Jerome: What happens when you cross a dog with a hen?
Oswald: I pass.
Jerome: Pooched eggs.

37

Johnny & Glenda

Johnny: Why didn't the other actors like working with the whale?
Glenda: I give up.
Johnny: He was always spouting off.

❖ ❖ ❖

Johnny: Why did Dr. Jekyll buy a sun lamp?
Glenda: I have no idea.
Johnny: He wanted to tan his hyde.

❖ ❖ ❖

Johnny: Why did the weird girl take lipstick and eye shadow to class?
Glenda: Who knows?

Johnny: Her teacher told her she had to take a makeup exam.

❖ ❖ ❖

Johnny: Why did the farmer name his pig Ink?
Glenda: I don't have the foggiest.
Johnny: It kept running out of the pen.

❖ ❖ ❖

Johnny: Why did the man keep staring at his belly?
Glenda: You tell me.
Johnny: His doctor told him to watch his weight.

❖ ❖ ❖

Johnny: Why did the goat eat fluorescent tubes?
Glenda: I can't guess.
Johnny: He wanted a light lunch.

❖ ❖ ❖

Johnny: Did you hear the story about the father snake asking the mother snake why Junior was so bouncy?
Glenda: No, what did she say?
Johnny: She told him it's because he's viper-active.

❖ ❖ ❖

Johnny: Why are donkeys so stubborn?
Glenda: I give up.
Johnny: Because they're mule-headed.

❖ ❖ ❖

Johnny: Why did King Neptune go to the doctor's office?
Glenda: That's a mystery.
Johnny: He had a herring problem.

❖ ❖ ❖

Johnny: Why did the exterminator hold his ears?
Glenda: I'm a blank.
Johnny: He couldn't stand to hear a moth bawl.

❖ ❖ ❖

Johnny: Why did the surfer cross the sea?
Glenda: It's unknown to me.
Johnny: To get to the other tide.

❖ ❖ ❖

Johnny: Why do hippos have gray skin?
Glenda: I'm in the dark.
Johnny: They have iron-poor blood.

❖ ❖ ❖

Johnny: Why does the sun get so big just before it goes down?
Glenda: I pass.
Johnny: It sucked up all that daylight.

38

More Daffy Definitions

Crime Wave: Piracy on the high seas.

❖ ❖ ❖

Farmer: A man with a sense of humus.

❖ ❖ ❖

Grouch: A man who spreads good cheer wherever he doesn't go.

❖ ❖ ❖

Heat Wave: What you get when you use a curling iron.

❖ ❖ ❖

Labor Contractions: Birthquakes.

❖ ❖ ❖

Mining: A vein pursuit.

❖ ❖ ❖

Moonlighting: The sun's other job.

❖ ❖ ❖

Noah: The first archeologist.

❖ ❖ ❖

Pedestrian: A father whose kids can drive.

❖ ❖ ❖

A Stupid Ruler: A ding-a-ling king.

❖ ❖ ❖

Tension: What the sergeant shouts to the troops.

❖ ❖ ❖

Tin: Not fat.

❖ ❖ ❖

Tips: Wages we pay other people's hired help.

❖ ❖ ❖

Toxic Waste: Your sister's cooking.

❖ ❖ ❖

Traffic Light: A little green light that changes to red as your car approaches.

❖ ❖ ❖

Wisecrack: An intelligent crevice.

❖ ❖ ❖

Zinc: What happens if you don't know how to zwim.

❖ ❖ ❖

Zinc: Where you put the dirty dishes.

39

Daphne & Darby

Daphne: What happens when two frogs go after the same fly?

Darby: I give up.

Daphne: They get tongue-tied.

❖ ❖ ❖

Daphne: What is yellow and writes?

Darby: I have no idea.

Daphne: A ball-point banana.

❖ ❖ ❖

Daphne: What word has five a's and no other vowel?

Darby: Who knows?

Daphne: Abracadabra.

❖ ❖ ❖

Daphne: What was the first weapon ever invented?
Darby: I don't have the foggiest.
Daphne: The Adam bomb.

❖ ❖ ❖

Daphne: What was your favorite class so far?
Darby: You tell me.
Daphne: The third grade. Didn't you spend two years there?

❖ ❖ ❖

Daphne: What stupid white whale bumps into a lot of ships?
Darby: I can't guess.
Daphne: Moby Dork.

❖ ❖ ❖

Daphne: What was wrong with the snobbish architect?
Darby: My mind is a blank.
Daphne: He was getting too big for his bridges.

❖ ❖ ❖

Daphne: What did the two whales say when they backed into each other?

Darby: I give up.
Daphne: All's whale that ends whale.

❖ ❖ ❖

Daphne: What is a sure way to find some money?
Darby: That's a mystery.
Daphne: Looking at the moon until it becomes a quarter.

❖ ❖ ❖

Daphne: What sea vessel had a barber for a captain?
Darby: I'm a blank.
Daphne: The clipper ship.

❖ ❖ ❖

Daphne: What's the difference between school and a mental hospital?
Darby: It's unknown to me.
Daphne: You have to show improvement to get out of the hospital.

❖ ❖ ❖

Daphne: What did the monster say after the evil scientist cloned him?
Darby: I'm in the dark.
Daphne: Nothing, he was beside himself.

40

Norm & Nancy

Norm: What is the strongest day in the week?
Nancy: I give up.
Norm: Sunday. The rest are weekdays.

❖ ❖ ❖

Norm: What kind of health food goes up and down?
Nancy: I have no idea.
Norm: Yo-yogurt.

❖ ❖ ❖

Norm: What did the chewing gum say to the shoe?
Nancy: Who knows?
Norm: I'm stuck on you.

❖ ❖ ❖

Norm: What does a duck wear to a formal dinner?

Nancy: I don't have the foggiest.

Norm: A duxedo.

❖ ❖ ❖

Norm: What did the little hog bring home from school?

Nancy: You tell me.

Norm: A repork card.

❖ ❖ ❖

Norm: What kind of fish can't wear clothes?

Nancy: My mind is a blank.

Norm: The bare-accuda.

❖ ❖ ❖

Norm: What's more accurate than a digital watch and able to tell time with a single bound?

Nancy: I give up.

Norm: Clock Kent.

❖ ❖ ❖

Norm: What happened after the two frogs got married?

Nancy: That's a mystery.

Norm: They lived hoppily ever after!

❖ ❖ ❖

Norm: What do you have when the whole world is covered with vegetables?

Nancy: I'm a blank.

Norm: Peas on earth.

❖ ❖ ❖

Norm: What keeps the moon from falling?

Nancy: It's unknown to me.

Norm: Its beams.

❖ ❖ ❖

Norm: What does the story of Jonah and the great fish teach us?

Nancy: I'm in the dark.

Norm: You can't keep a good man down.

❖ ❖ ❖

Norm: What do they call basketball in Honolulu?

Nancy: I pass.

Norm: Hula hoop.

❖ ❖ ❖

Norm: What's the best way to describe an out-of-shape marathoner?
Nancy: You've got me guessing.
Norm: A sore loser.

❖ ❖ ❖

Norm: What are the worst five years in the life of a Smogarian?
Nancy: How should I know?
Norm: Third grade.

41

Wardle & Weller

Wardle: What kind of hangers do mountains use in their closets?
Weller: I give up.
Wardle: Cliff-hangers.

❖ ❖ ❖

Wardle: What do little whales learn in school?
Weller: I have no idea.
Wardle: Their A, B, Seas.

❖ ❖ ❖

Wardle: What do you call ten law students standing ear to ear?
Weller: Who knows?
Wardle: A wind tunnel.

❖ ❖ ❖

Wardle: What did Robin Hood shoot with on wet days?
Weller: I don't have the foggiest.
Wardle: His rain-bow.

❖ ❖ ❖

Wardle: What's the best job for a midget?
Weller: You tell me.
Wardle: A short-order cook.

❖ ❖ ❖

Wardle: What was the name of Mr. Walnut's girlfriend?
Weller: I can't guess.
Wardle: Hazel Nut.

❖ ❖ ❖

Wardle: What do you call two mids side by side?
Weller: My mind is a blank.
Wardle: Pyramids.

❖ ❖ ❖

Wardle: What's the favorite Christmas song in the rain forest?
Weller: I give up.
Wardle: Jungle Bells.

❖ ❖ ❖

Wardle: What did the preacher say at the pickle wedding?
Weller: That's a mystery.
Wardle: Dilly Beloved, we are gathered here together . . .

❖ ❖ ❖

Wardle: What man in the Bible had no parents?
Weller: I'm a blank.
Wardle: Joshua, the son of Nun.

❖ ❖ ❖

Wardle: What do you call wooden comedians?
Weller: It's unknown to me.
Wardle: The Tree Stooges.

❖ ❖ ❖

Wardle: What can most Smogarian kids do by the age of 12?
Weller: I'm in the dark.
Wardle: Wave bye-bye.

42

Rod & Deena

Rod: What do you break when you move it?
Deena: I give up.
Rod: Silence.

❖ ❖ ❖

Rod: What do you call a bird who tattles to the lifeguard?
Deena: I have no idea.
Rod: A pool pigeon.

❖ ❖ ❖

Rod: What does a pig carpenter use to drive in nails?
Deena: Who knows?
Rod: A hammer.

❖ ❖ ❖

Rod: What do you call an automobile that's packed in a crate?
Deena: I don't have the foggiest.
Rod: A boxcar.

❖ ❖ ❖

Rod: What do you think about that new math program?
Deena: You tell me.
Rod: It's a nice addition.

❖ ❖ ❖

Rod: What does a baby computer call its father?
Deena: I can't guess.
Rod: Data.

❖ ❖ ❖

Rod: Cross a flea with a rabbit and what do you get?
Deena: My mind is a blank.
Rod: Bugs Bunny.

❖ ❖ ❖

Rod: What do you think of the allergy season?
Deena: It's nothing to sneeze at.

❖ ❖ ❖

Rod: What do you get when you cross some grain and shoe polish?

Deena: That's a mystery.

Rod: Rice and shine.

❖ ❖ ❖

Rod: What do you call a bunch of singing bed sheets?

Deena: I'm a blank.

Rod: The Linen Sisters.

❖ ❖ ❖

Rod: What should you do if your haystack gets wet?

Deena: It's unknown to me.

Rod: Bale it out.

❖ ❖ ❖

Rod: What breaks but never falls, and what falls but never breaks?

Deena: I'm in the dark.

Rod: Dawn breaks and never falls, and night falls but never breaks.

❖ ❖ ❖

Rod: What do competitive surfers call the wave that wins them a championship?
Deena: I pass.
Rod: A title wave.

❖ ❖ ❖

Rod: What was Eve's telephone number in the Garden of Eden?
Deena: You've got me guessing.
Rod: I think it was Adam-812.

❖ ❖ ❖

Rod: What simple affliction brought about the death of Samson?
Deena: How should I know?
Rod: Fallen arches.

❖ ❖ ❖

Rod: What should you do if a rodent faints?
Deena: Search me.
Rod: Give it mouse-to-mouse rescucitation.

43

Toby & Topsy

Toby: What's the best way to get rid of a 100-pound worm?

Topsy: I give up.

Toby: Invite a 1000-pound robin over for breakfast.

❖ ❖ ❖

Toby: What do you call hamburgers that pout?

Topsy: I have no idea.

Toby: Fry babies.

❖ ❖ ❖

Toby: What famous pig was a great psychologist?

Topsy: Who knows?

Toby: Pigmund Freud.

❖ ❖ ❖

Toby: What does a dog do that a man steps into?
Topsy: I don't have the foggiest.
Toby: Pants.

❖ ❖ ❖

Toby: What do you give a seasick elephant?
Topsy: You tell me.
Toby: Lots of space.

❖ ❖ ❖

Toby: What are the friendliest things in the Arctic?
Topsy: I can't guess.
Toby: Nicebergs.

❖ ❖ ❖

Toby: What kind of bugs hang around bowling alleys?
Topsy: My mind is a blank.
Toby: Bowl weevils.

❖ ❖ ❖

Toby: What do you call the spine of a hog?
Topsy: I give up.
Toby: A piggyback.

❖ ❖ ❖

Toby: What should you say to a conceited undertaker?
Topsy: That's a mystery.
Toby: Come down off your high hearse!

❖ ❖ ❖

Toby: What do you call a pancake that you can't eat?
Topsy: I'm a blank.
Toby: A flop-jack.

❖ ❖ ❖

Toby: What word of only three syllables contains 26 letters?
Topsy: It's unknown to me.
Toby: The alphabet.

❖ ❖ ❖

Toby: What did the boy license plate say to the girl license plate?
Topsy: I'm in the dark.
Toby: You're a cute number.

44

Bob & Esther

Bob: What do you get when you cross a lawyer with a snake?

Esther: I give up.

Bob: Trick question! Even snakes have standards.

❖ ❖ ❖

Bob: What did one blackbird say to the other blackbird?

Esther: I have no idea.

Bob: Crow up!

❖ ❖ ❖

Bob: What do you call elephants who ride in jet airplanes?

Esther: Who knows?

Bob: Passengers.

❖ ❖ ❖

Bob: What stays the same age year after year?

Esther: I don't have the foggiest.

Bob: A woman over 40.

❖ ❖ ❖

Bob: What do you call a story about a cow that has a fairy godmother?

Esther: You tell me.

Bob: A dairy tale.

❖ ❖ ❖

Bob: What famous western sheriff started a chain of hotels?

Esther: I can't guess.

Bob: Hyatt Earp.

❖ ❖ ❖

Bob: What do you think of tennis?

Esther: My mind is a blank.

Bob: It's a racket.

❖ ❖ ❖

Bob: What did the Arab do when he saw a mouse?
Esther: I give up.
Bob: He let out a sheik.

❖ ❖ ❖

Bob: What did Aesop's wife say after Aesop came home late?
Esther: It's a mystery.
Bob: That's a pretty fable excuse.

❖ ❖ ❖

Bob: What kind of a boat does a dentist sail?
Esther: I'm a blank.
Bob: A Tooth Ferry.

❖ ❖ ❖

Bob: What happened to Lassie after he ate a cantaloupe?
Esther: It's unknown to me.
Bob: He felt melon-collie.

❖ ❖ ❖

Bob: What kind of pollution hurts foxes the most?
Esther: I'm in the dark.
Bob: Foxic waste.

❖ ❖ ❖

Bob: What crazy motive led to the invention of the railroad?

Esther: I pass.

Bob: The locomotive.

❖ ❖ ❖

Bob: What is the difference between a mirror and a chatterbox?

Esther: You've got me guessing.

Bob: A mirror reflects without speaking; a chatterbox speaks without reflecting.

❖ ❖ ❖

Bob: Did you hear about the Sunday school teacher who asked her class what they knew about Adam's wife, Eve?

Esther: No, what happened?

Bob: One of her students said, "They named Christmas Eve after her."

45

Barnaby & Bailey

Barnaby: What is yellow and pink?
Bailey: I give up.
Barnaby: A blushing banana.

❖ ❖ ❖

Barnaby: What has three feet, three eyes, and two bills?
Bailey: I have no idea.
Barnaby: A duck with spare parts.

❖ ❖ ❖

Barnaby: What do you get when you cross a Smogarian with an ape?
Bailey: Who knows?
Barnaby: A retarded ape.

❖ ❖ ❖

Barnaby: What do you get when you cross a lawyer with an ape?

Bailey: I don't have the foggiest.

Barnaby: You still get an ape.

❖ ❖ ❖

Barnaby: What position would a midget play on your baseball team?

Bailey: You tell me.

Barnaby: Shortstop.

❖ ❖ ❖

Barnaby: What is a falsehood?

Bailey: I can't guess.

Barnaby: A falsehood is an undercover cop pretending to be a crook.

❖ ❖ ❖

Barnaby: What do you think about all the new court shows?

Bailey: I haven't reached a verdict yet.

❖ ❖ ❖

Barnaby: What is the difference between a jackrabbit and a duck?

Bailey: I give up.

Barnaby: One goes quick on his legs, and the other goes quack on her eggs.

❖ ❖ ❖

Barnaby: What do bees say on hot days?
Bailey: That's a mystery.
Barnaby: Swarm, isn't it?

❖ ❖ ❖

Barnaby: What happened to the man who sat up all night wondering where the sun went when it set?
Bailey: I'm a blank.
Barnaby: It finally dawned on him.

❖ ❖ ❖

Barnaby: What is that which Adam never saw or possessed, yet left two for each of his children?
Bailey: It's unknown to me.
Barnaby: Parents.

❖ ❖ ❖

Barnaby: What do you call a bear that got caught in the rain?
Bailey: I'm in the dark.
Barnaby: A drizzly bear.

46

More School Daze

Principal: I've been told you're advocating a world revolution.

Teacher: All I said was, there's a revolution of the earth every year.

❖ ❖ ❖

A kid in my class is so dumb that he once appeared on Lifestyles of the Dull and Stupid.

❖ ❖ ❖

A principal called the mother of one of his students. He said, "I have good news and bad news. The bad news is your son thinks he's a frog."

"What's the good news?" asked the mother.

"The good news is I think we licked the fly problem in the cafeteria.

❖ ❖ ❖

The crime in our school is so bad that when the teacher says "Line up," she means a police lineup.

❖ ❖ ❖

A kid in my class is so dumb that he paid $50 for a tattoo in the shape of a freckle.

❖ ❖ ❖

He's a few french fries short of a Happy Meal.

❖ ❖ ❖

A Sunday school teacher asked her class to draw a picture illustrating a Bible story. One paper handed in contained a picture of a big car. An old man, with long whiskers flying in the breeze, was driving. A man and a woman were seated in the back of the car. Puzzled, the teacher asked little Johnny to explain his drawing. "Why, that is God driving Adam and Eve out of the Garden of Eden."

❖ ❖ ❖

Teacher: What parable in the Bible do you like best?

Student: The one about the fellow that loafs and fishes.

❖ ❖ ❖

Teacher: Where was Solomon's temple?

Student: On the side of his head.

❖ ❖ ❖

Teacher: In our lesson today we have talked about the burnt offerings offered in the Old Testament. Why don't we have burnt offerings today?

Student: On account of air pollution.

❖ ❖ ❖

The teacher handed out the test papers and told the children they could start answering the questions.

She noticed little Billy sitting with his head bowed, his hands over his face. She approached him.

"Don't you feel well?" she inquired.

"Oh, I'm fine, teacher. Maybe it's unconstitutional, but I always pray before a test!"

❖ ❖ ❖

Sunday school teacher: Can anyone tell me the story of Adam and Eve?

Little girl: First God created Adam. Then He looked at him and said, "I think I could do better if I tried again." So He created Eve.

❖ ❖ ❖

A little boy, just back from Sunday school, asked his father if Noah had a wife.

"All the time, questions, questions, questions," replied the father. "Of course he did: Joan of Arc."

47

Boyd & Margie

Boyd: What kind of oil has the worst manners?
Margie: I give up.
Boyd: Crude oil.

❖ ❖ ❖

Boyd: What's the grouchiest kind of wind?
Margie: I have no idea.
Boyd: A crosswind.

❖ ❖ ❖

Boyd: What do you get when you cross a bee and a gorilla?
Margie: Who knows?
Boyd: Sting Kong.

❖ ❖ ❖

Boyd: What loses its head every morning?
Margie: I don't have the foggiest.
Boyd: A pillow.

❖ ❖ ❖

Boyd: Why do they bury a man on the side of a hill?
Margie: I can't guess.
Boyd: He's dead.

❖ ❖ ❖

Boyd: What does a tornado and the school bully have in common?
Margie: My mind is a blank.
Boyd: They're both full of wind.

❖ ❖ ❖

Boyd: What do you get when you cross Old MacDonald and a pickle?
Margie: I give up.
Boyd: The farmer in the dill.

❖ ❖ ❖

Boyd: What do you call a tiny telephone?
Margie: That's a mystery.
Boyd: A micro-phone.

❖ ❖ ❖

Boyd: What do you say just before you steal a bottle of glue?
Margie: I'm a blank.
Boyd: Stick 'em up.

❖ ❖ ❖

Boyd: What does an ice-skater do when he wants to get inside a house?
Margie: It's unknown to me.
Boyd: He rinks the doorbell.

❖ ❖ ❖

Boyd: What makes a meteor shower?
Margie: I'm in the dark.
Boyd: Good hygiene habits.

❖ ❖ ❖

Boyd: What did Adam and Eve do when they were expelled from Eden?
Margie: I pass.
Boyd: They raised Cain.

❖ ❖ ❖

Boyd: What do they do with the church flowers after Sunday services?
Margie: You've got me guessing.
Boyd: They take them to the people who are sick after the sermons.

❖ ❖ ❖

Boyd: What is the difference between a cat and a frog?

Margie: How should I know?

Boyd: The cat has only nine lives; a frog croaks every minute.

Other Books by Bob Phillips

World's Greatest Collection of Clean Jokes

The Return of the Good Clean Jokes

The World's Greatest Collection of Heavenly Humor

The World's Greatest Collection of Riddles and Daffy Definitions

The World's Greatest Collection of Knock, Knock Jokes and Tongue Twisters

The Best of the Good Clean Jokes

Wit and Wisdom

Humor Is Tremendous

The All-New Clean Joke Book

Good Clean Jokes for Kids

The Encyclopedia of Good Clean Jokes

Ultimate Good Clean Jokes for Kids

Awesome Good Clean Jokes for Kids

More Awesome Good Clean Jokes for Kids

Wacky Good Clean Jokes for Kids

Nutty Good Clean Jokes for Kids

Loony Good Clean Jokes for Kids

Crazy Good Clean Jokes for Kids

Goofy Good Clean Jokes for Kids

Bible Brainteasers

The Great Bible Challenge

The Awesome Book of Bible Trivia

How Can I Be Sure?

Anger Is a Choice

Redi-Reference

Redi-Reference Daily Bible-Reading Plan

The Delicate Art of Dancing with Porcupines

God's Hand over Hume

Praise Is a Three-Lettered Word—Joy

Friendship, Love & Laughter

Phillips' Book of Great Quotes & Funny Sayings

The All-American Quote Book

Bible Olympics

Big Book—The Bible—Questions and Answers

The Unofficial Liberal Joke Book

What to Do Until the Psychiatrist Comes

For information on how to purchase any of the above books, contact your local bookstore or send a self-addressed stamped envelope to:
Family Services
P.O. Box 9363
Fresno, CA 93702